GET SET...GO!

JAMES R. SHERMAN

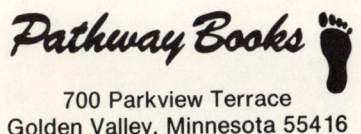

700 Parkview Terrace
Golden Valley, Minnesota 55416

Other Books by James R. Sherman

How to Overcome a Bad Back
Stop Procrastinating—DO IT!
REJECTION
Escape to the Gunflint

GET SET ... GO!

First Edition, October, 1983
Copyright © 1983 James R. Sherman
All Rights Reserved

Library of Congress Number
83-062907

International Standard Book Number
0-935538-05-4

Pathway Books
700 Parkview Terrace
Golden Valley, Minnesota 55416
(612) 377-1521

To: *my son* Chris, *with special thanks.*

CONTENTS

PREFACE   ix

INTRODUCTION TO PLANNING

The Definition of Planning	2
Types of Planning	3
The Seven Steps of Planning	3
The Nature of Planning	5
The Benefits of Planning	5
Dangers in Planning	6
Why People Don't Plan	7
Planning Models	9
There's More to Come	10

INVESTIGATION

Know Yourself	11
Know Your World	15
Conceptual Blocks	18
Summary	20

DECISION

Alternatives and Choices	21
Goals and Objectives	26
Planning Assumptions	27
How to Develop Goals and Objectives	28
Conceptual Blockbusting	30
How to Write Your Goals and Objectives	31
Summary	32

ORGANIZATION

Priorities	33
Performance Measures	36
Have You Arrived?	37
The Element of Risk	38
Summary	39

PREPARATION

Get Set To Go	41
What Makes Good Planning	45
How To Be A Good Planner	46
Causes of Failure and How To Avoid Them	48
Planning for Contingencies	51
Luck and Planning	52
Summary	52

IMPLEMENTATION

Making It Work	53
Summary	59

A FINAL WORD

BIBLIOGRAPHY	63
INDEX	65

PREFACE

On your marks...
Get set...Get set...Get set...
I've met lots of people who never get beyond that step. They feel unprepared and anxious about some future event, and that frustrates them. So they go to workshops, seminars, and retreats, to try to feel better about themselves and their role in an uncharted future. And a lot of them come away from those sessions with great expectations.

You might be one of those well-intentioned people. I know I was. But usually, my expectations lasted only a week or so. And then I'd find myself back in my same old rut.

It wasn't that I didn't want to get better at what I was doing, or that I was ignoring what lay ahead. I just didn't know how or where to start. I didn't have a plan, and I didn't know how to make one. At the same time, I saw lots of other people who were in the same boat I was. If you've been there, you know how bad it can be. It's terrible.

People can get very frustrated when they want something they know would be good for them and yet they can't have it. To have a worthwhile goal and not be able to reach it. To want to climb the ladder of success and not even be able to find the ladder.

They keep experiencing periods of exhilaration and the same thing happens over and over again. They get all psyched up and loaded for bear, and then everything crumbles in a pile and they're left with nothing. They feel ashamed, frustrated, impotent, and just plain dumb. At least I did.

Then I decided I didn't want to feel that way any longer. I wanted to channel all my dreams, goals, and ambitions into reality. I wanted to get from point A, where I was, to point B, where I wanted to be. So I learned how to plan.

I not only found out how to do it, I learned how to do it pretty well. For several years I worked as a management consultant to colleges and universities, and I taught them how to plan. Everything from annual budgets to daily operating routines. They found out that planning wasn't hard at all. I think you'll discover the same thing.

I've tried to put together everything I learned about planning in a short, concise, and comprehensive book. It should be just the thing to get you started on this important aspect of your life.

So...

On your mark...

Get set...

GO!

JAMES R. SHERMAN, Ph.D.

INTRODUCTION TO PLANNING

"A journey of a thousand miles begins with a single step."

You can bet your sweet bippy that the Chinese philosopher who coined that phrase didn't just leap over the edge of the Great Wall and take off. Anyone traveling that far is going to have some idea of where they're headed. If they don't, they're going to be like Alice in Wonderland.

"Cheshire-Puss,"...said Alice, "would you tell me, please, which way I ought to go from here?"

"That depends a good deal on where you want to get to," said the Cat.

"I don't much care where—" said Alice.

"Then it doesn't matter which way you go," said the Cat.

"—so long as I get *somewhere*," Alice added as an explanation.

"Oh, you're sure to do that," said the Cat, "if you only walk long enough."

People like Alice, who don't know where they're going, are probably frustrated. That's natural. Especially if they want to do something they haven't been able to do before, or become someone they've always wanted to be, but don't know how to make the change. And if they can't make any progress toward things that mean a lot to them, their frustration is going to get worse.

If you're frustrated, it can put a damper on everything you do and slow you down to a crawl. It can also make you feel depressed, because you don't have anything definite to do to get going again.

This is especially true if you don't have a plan to follow or a definite goal to work toward.

To start feeling better again, you've got to see where you are, decide where you want to go, and then do what's necessary to get there with the least amount of trouble. Simple steps, but some that a lot of folks find hard to take.

The key to success lies in planning, and the promise it holds is fantastic. By just doing a few simple tasks, you can keep from running around like a chicken with its head cut off, and march off instead to a happy future.

Planning is a proven way of becoming more productive. But it's not a cure-all. It's only good if it works for you.

If you're completely satisfied with your current level of productivity and don't want to go through the process of planning, then go no further. But if you feel your days pass with little to show for them, then this book is for you. You're going to get a lot out of it, and it's going to help you get a lot more out of life.

That's what this book is all about. And here's what planning is all about.

THE DEFINITION OF PLANNING

Planning is the design of a hoped-for future and the development of effective steps for bringing it about.

Planning helps you identify opportunities and problems and shows you how to take care of them within a set period of time. It forces you to make realistic assessments of where you are now and where you'd like to be in the future. It helps you develop and implement specific strategies that will get you where you want to go. Planning makes you think ahead in terms of facts instead of fantasies.

Planning changes you into the kind of person you want to be by giving you the power to control your destiny. It's a rational, systematic method of decision making and problem solving that combines experience, knowledge, and skill with goals and objectives. It helps you see the risks you have to take when you chart a course into an unknown future.

Planning starts when you figure out where you are and then decide you want something better. It picks up speed as you collect data, develop proper strategies and alternatives, choose a course of action, and carry out a series of tasks. It's the same procedure no matter what type of planning you're doing.

TYPES OF PLANNING

There are two major types of planning. One deals with future events that haven't happened yet. There's not much you can do to control these events, you just have to be ready to deal with them when they arrive. A new job, a geographical move, a change in the weather, or the arrival of a baby are some of the things that call for future planning.

The other type of planning deals with changes in your present circumstances. You want to lose weight, take a trip, or change your job. You can control your destiny and effect the change you want by developing a plan of action.

Besides the two types of planning, there are a couple of different ways in which it's done. One is the *follow the leader* approach where you try to copy what others have done in the past. The other approach is called *analytical planning*. It means studying a problem you feel you have, checking out alternative courses of action, and selecting the most promising solution.

The steps you follow in the planning process will generally be the same, regardless of the type of planning you choose.

THE SEVEN STEPS OF PLANNING

Here are the seven major steps of planning.

ASSESSMENT

You get an uneasy feeling about who you are and what you're doing. You look at where you are in life and you see a need as well as a desire to change.

COMMITMENT

The need for change leads to a commitment on your part to accomplish that change. You recognize that planning is something you have to do and then you set aside time to do it.

INVESTIGATION

You study every aspect of your life and try to remember what you've done before. You look at your present situation and list the skills you have to offer and the handicaps you have to bear. You examine the relationships you've had with other people, especially if you've had to compete against others to get ahead. You figure out what it's going to cost you to plan, and you identify the risks you're going to have to take.

DECISION

You come up with as many different choices as you can. Then, based on a gut feeling of what you think is going to happen in the future, you decide what you want to do and when you want to get it done.

ORGANIZATION

You pick the planning strategy that will best serve your needs and at the same time let you reach your goals and objectives. You set priorities, establish timetables, and figure out how you're going to evaluate your progress.

PREPARATION

As soon as you've decided on your plan of action, you gather up everything you need to carry it out, including the suggestions found in this book. You fine-tune your plan and get ready to deal with anything that can go wrong.

IMPLEMENTATION

As you carry out your plan, you see how well things are going by measuring your performance against your original expectations. If you run into problems, you shift gears and come up with other ways of reaching your goals and objectives.

These seven steps are easy to follow if you have a good understanding of the nature of planning.

THE NATURE OF PLANNING

Effective planning is flexible and allows for change and modification. Overplanning, with its rigid deadlines and precise expectations, is just as bad as underplanning.

Planning, by its very nature, will change your image of reality and your vision of the future.

You can use planning as a tool for analyzing your expectations and chances for success. Planning can also tell you how far you need to go to reach a goal you really want.

The key to planning is to get a glimpse of the future. Not an idealistic notion of what you want it to be, but a realistic vision of what you think it can and will be. Walt Disney, Henry Ford, and the Wright brothers are some of the great people who went through life with visions of what could be. They were successful because they made their visions come true. They obviously knew the benefits of planning.

THE BENEFITS OF PLANNING

Planning has so many benefits it's hard to mention them all. A few stand out, however, and should be mentioned here.

* Planning makes you think ahead.

* It helps coordinate your efforts.

* It helps you develop performance standards so you'll know how well you're doing.

* It helps clarify your goals and objectives.

* It prepares you for sudden and unexpected developments.

* It helps you see how different activities interact.

* It keeps you from reaching a dead-end in work, creativity, and happiness.

Planning makes you more efficient and effective. It improves your morale, your attitudes, and the way you work with others. When you've planned for the future, you feel more secure about the days ahead and of your relationships with other people. You know if you're on the right track, because you can measure your progress against milestones that you establish.

Planning isn't always a bed of roses. Sometimes, it can even get you into trouble.

DANGERS IN PLANNING

There are a lot of benefits in planning, but there are also some dangers. Here are some of the pitfalls to watch out for.

LACK OF SPONTANEITY

If you're inflexible in your planning, you can miss out on a lot of opportunities that happen on the spur of the moment. You can't plan to be spontaneous. That's a contradiction in terms.

FEAR OF THE UNKNOWN

If you put too much faith in your plan, you may be afraid to break out and try something new. Your fear of the unknown can shut you down completely.

LACK OF GROWTH

If you follow your plan too closely, you can wipe out the stimulation and excitement you need to keep growing. You must be flexible enough to entertain new ideas, gain new knowledge, and change to new methods when the time is right.

PSYCHOLOGICAL DISTRESS

Planning can turn you into a well-organized slave of methods and procedures. And that can lead to a lack of creativity and an inability to innovate, resulting in frustration, unhappiness, and shortsightedness.

HUNG UP ON METHOD

Little by little, you can get hung up on methods, techniques, and procedures to where they take over the entire goal-seeking process. *How* it's done gets to be more important than *whether* it's done.

You probably know people who go through life with a road map and a list. They can't do anything that isn't a part of their great master plan for the future. Their plans aren't necessarily unhealthy, but when they fall in love with their plan, it's a sign of a real neurosis.

To avoid the dangers in planning, you have to have enough faith in yourself to be able to change your plans whenever it's necessary. You should also keep an open mind and never let yourself get addicted to your plans.

Too much of any good thing can be bad for you, and planning is no exception. There are, however, some shortsighted people who see only the dangers in planning. They don't want anything to do with it no matter how good it is.

WHY PEOPLE DON'T PLAN

People don't plan because of their attitudes. If they don't like what's going on, they'll do everything they can to sabotage the planning process.

ATTITUDES AGAINST PLANNING

There are as many attitudes against planning as there are people who don't want to try it. Here are some of the more familiar reasons why people refuse to plan.
"Planning is too time consuming."
"There's too much hard work involved in planning."
"The future is too uncertain for planning to have any value."
"I don't like or understand the planning process."
"We should live for today and not think about the future."
"People live by intuition and not by planning."

There are several other obstacles besides attitudes that can foul up the planning process. Here are some of them.

OTHER OBSTACLES

* Planning efforts can be shot down if people don't have the knowledge and skill needed to carry them out.
* The fear of failure, the fear of making a mistake, and the fear of taking a risk are all obstacles to planning.
* People with an overriding desire for security and order and no appetite for chaos, can't tolerate the ambiguity of an unknown future. They're so obsessed with the present that they never take time to plan.
* People who prefer to judge ideas rather than generate them, and who find no challenge in the problems they're faced with, are not about to start planning.
* Overmotivation, excessive zeal, and the need for immediate gratification keep many people from planning.
* People who can't distinguish reality from fantasy have a hard time planning for the future.
* People who are against planning are generally afraid of its implications, even when they don't know what they are. They don't want to change their normal operating routines, because they're nice and comfortable in those routines.
* Being opposed to planning is, for some people, a subtle way of asserting their individuality. It also helps them escape the responsibility that comes with planning.

Now that you've seen both sides of planning, here's something that will help you understand the planning process.

PLANNING MODELS

Planning models are miniature representations of what goes on in the real world. They help you see, in your mind's eye, what the planning process is all about.

Planning models provide the framework around which you can build any plan, no matter how complicated or long-lasting it might be. It can be a large, corporate plan, or a simple day-to-day plan for trying to reach your personal goals and objectives. Once you're accustomed to the framework, you can apply it wherever you want.

The planning process is described all through this book by an *inside-out* planning model. It's called inside-out because the primary focus is on you. In contrast, an *outside-in* model emphasizes the world you live in. You come second. Here's a brief description of both models.

INSIDE-OUT PLANNING

Inside-out planning is tailored to what you're able to do, are doing now, and have enough confidence to do in the days ahead. It lets you see what's possible when you focus on things you're good at and enjoy doing, instead of taking chances on hypothetical estimates of the world around you.

Inside-out planning lets you figure out what you need to do as an individual to reach your short-range and long-term goals and objectives. It calls for a lot of self-appraisal. But that makes it more reliable. Because the things that make you what you are, are more substantial and last a lot longer than things that describe the world you live in.

OUTSIDE-IN PLANNING

Outside-in planning is the opposite of inside-out planning. It makes use of what other people think is happening now or is going to happen in the future. It calls for a continuous analysis of outside trends, conditions, and other environmental factors.

You usually run into a time lag when you try to get information for outside-in planning. That's because outside-in planning only takes into consideration things that other people already know about. It doesn't make use of information that isn't generally available. So if you're going to use the outside-in model, you'll always be a step behind.

The inside-out and outside-in planning models provide just a taste of what lies ahead in this book.

THERE'S MORE TO COME

By now, you've taken the first two steps in planning. You saw the need for getting a handle on your future, and you made a commitment to start planning for it. You'll get to know the other steps in the planning process as you go through the rest of this book.

Chapter 2 will introduce you to the process of investigation and analysis so you can learn more about yourself and the world around you.

In Chapter 3, you'll decide what it is you want to do, and then figure out how to get it done.

In Chapter 4, you'll do everything necessary to organize your plan and get it ready for implementation.

Chapter 5 will give you some tips on how to plan. It will tell you how to be a good planner and how to avoid problems that can come up along the way.

Chapter 6 will tell you how to put your plan in operation and move forward into the future. It will top off the book by presenting eighteen separate strategies for approaching your task in the best way possible.

So if you're ready to change your life, turn to Chapter 2 and start gathering the information you need to build your plans for the future.

INVESTIGATION

There are two major activities in planning. The first is to figure out where you are, and the second is to decide where you want to be. The material in this chapter will help you find out where you are.

To be successful in planning, you have to know as much as you can about yourself and the world you live in. What you learn in those two areas will form the basis for the rest of your planning activities.

KNOW YOURSELF

A balanced viewpoint is important, so you should look at both your strengths *and* your weaknesses.

This is really a *mirror, mirror on the wall* exercise.

STRENGTHS

Take a sheet of paper and divide it in half. On one half, write down all the *things you're good at*. Include things you've done that have earned you praise from other people. List things that give you a lot of self-satisfaction, like making money, speaking in public, playing a musical instrument, taking part in sporting events, building objects with your hands, or selling products or ideas to other people.

Include intangible things like values, work attitudes, willingness to accept risk, the way you feel about yourself, and other attributes that set you apart from the crowd.

On the other half of the sheet, put down *things you enjoy doing* whether you're good at them or not. Cover things like hiking, camping, traveling, playing tennis, managing money, closing a sale, completing a report, or meeting new people. Let yourself go and put down anything that comes to mind.

As you put your list together, try to focus on specific areas of strength. Here are the ones that are going to have the greatest impact on your future success: (a) your health, (b) your intelligence, (c) your experiences, (d) your motivation, (e) your talents and skills, and (f) your personal appearance. Figure out what you need to do to reinforce each of these areas and make them stronger.

You'll find examples of strengths in Figure 1.

FIGURE 1

EXAMPLES OF STRENGTHS

Things I'm good at

1. Speaking in public
2. Playing a musical instrument
3. Building objects with my hands
4. Selling products or ideas to other people
5. Working hard

Things I like to do

6. Meet new people
7. Accept risk
8. Travel
9. Close a sale
10. Call on customers

Other Strengths

11. Excellent health
12. Intelligent
13. Lots of experience in my field

If you have a hard time identifying your strengths, look for outside opinions from people you can trust, especially those who know you well. Be objective, and don't just look for qualities you wish you had or ignore those you think are not important.

WEAKNESSES

Take another sheet of paper and divide it in half like you did before. On one half, put down activities that are a part of your job or personal life that *you're not very good at*, or that you just can't seem to develop a knack for doing. Don't put down things like mountain climbing or sailboat racing if you've never done them before.

Personal habits, like laziness, indifference, and lack of concentration, can also threaten your planning success. So can an inability to communicate. Be sure to put them down as weaknesses.

On the other half of the page, put down *things you don't like to do*. Include things like getting up early, writing up sales reports, staying in the office, or talking on the telephone. Put down anything you'd avoid doing if you could.

Include physical as well as mental shortcomings that keep you from moving ahead. Be honest with yourself. It's better to identify problem areas before you get started than to discover them when you're hopelessly locked in an impossible journey.

You'll find a list of weaknesses in Figure 2.

It will help if you focus on specific areas like you did when you made your list of strengths. The areas you want to be sure to cover are (a) your friends, (b) your family, (c) your job, (d) your business associates, and (e) the social environment you find yourself in.

COMPARE YOUR LISTS

Here's where your two lists start to cross over. You might be very good at something, but not like to do it. Or you may enjoy doing something but have no talent for it at all. Let your emotions decide where to put the item. If you like to do it, list it among your

> **FIGURE 2**
> **EXAMPLES OF WEAKNESSES**
>
> **Things I'm not very good at**
>   1. Handling other people's complaints
>   2. Taking examinations
>   3. Concentrating on difficult tasks
>   4. Controlling my temper
>   5. Coping with physical or emotional stress
>
> **Things I don't like to do**
>   6. Get up early
>   7. Write up sales reports
>   8. Stay in the office
>   9. Talk on the telephone
>   10. Busy work
>
> **Other Weaknesses**
>   11. Lack of personal growth
>   12. Little net worth

strengths even if you're not very good at it. And if you don't like to do it, put it down with your weaknesses.

There's a simple reason for arranging things according to the way you feel about them. You're more inclined to develop a skill for things you like to do than for things you don't like to do. So even though you don't have the skills now, it's possible that you'll develop them in the future if it involves something you're interested in.

Now combine the two halves of each list. You'll probably find a lot of duplication, because the things you like to do are usually those you're good at. And the ones you aren't very good at are usually those you don't like to do.

QUIZ YOURSELF

The success of your planning efforts will depend a lot on how much you know and are able to find out about yourself. But if you're like many people, you might find it hard to come up with a list of your strengths and weaknesses.

Here are some questions that will help you in your investigation. Your answers should give you a better idea of where you are and what you want to be. If you spend enough time with each of them, they should give you some pretty good answers.

1. Where am I now? What's my position in the world around me? How well am I performing?
2. What results can I expect from what I'm doing now? What am I growing and what will I harvest?
3. What do I want to be? Where do I want to go? What are my goals and objectives? What is my philosophy of life?
4. How can I get where I want to go? What tools and resources am I going to need to get there? What should I change? What should I keep the same?
5. How will I know when I've arrived at my destination?

Your answers to these questions will give you a better understanding of your capabilities and limitations. They'll also help you develop a realistic idea of the options that are open to you.

Another helpful step you can take is to look back over your history of successes and failures. Write down the most significant events that have happened to you in the past three to five years, and be able to tell other people why they mean so much to you.

If you're still having a hard time figuring out who and what you are, you might want to look at another one of my books called ***REJECTION***. It covers most of the concerns that are discussed here, except it goes into much greater detail. It's listed in the bibliography.

KNOW YOUR WORLD

You have to know where you are in the world you live in before you can successfully plan for the future. It helps if you look at the opportunities and threats that you run into from time to time.

OPPORTUNITIES

Take a third sheet of paper and write down every opportunity you can think of that's open to you. List the ones that are easy to get, along with those that call for a lot of hard work. If your competition is weak, put that down as an opportunity. If you're trying to sell something, and you have a lot of potential customers, put that down on the same list.

Remember to put down the intangibles, like your relationship with other people, the part of the country you live in, or your role in a social or business group.

Put down everything you can think of that might help you be successful in whatever you decide to do. But in making your list, be sure you only put down the opportunities you really want or would be happy in pursuing.

A list of potential opportunities is shown in Figure 3.

FIGURE 3

EXAMPLES OF OPPORTUNITIES

Things that can help me be successful

1. Little or no competition
2. Lots of customers
3. Good product line
4. Ideal economic conditions
5. Lots of friends
6. Membership in a business association
7. Rapidly growing community
8. Good working conditions
9. Helpful business associates
10. Strong family support

THREATS

Take a fourth sheet of paper and make a list of all the threats that face you. Put down everything you can think of that could frustrate your efforts or slow down your progress.

Some of the things you list as opportunities, like your competition, can also be considered threats if they're stronger than you. Your lack of expertise in areas where you're working can be a threat. A very small clientele can pose a threat if there are several people like you trying to get their business. The current economic situation can be either a threat or an opportunity, depending on what you're trying to do.

Figure 4 illustrates some of the threats you might face.

FIGURE 4

EXAMPLES OF THREATS

Things that can keep me from being successful

1. Poor distribution channels
2. Rising cost of shipping
3. Number of dissatisfied customers
4. Limited transportation facilities
5. Shortage of available cash
6. Lack of time
7. Rising cost of space
8. High cost of education
9. Limited opportunity for advancement
10. Oppressive governmental regulations

Use the examples in Figures 3 and 4 to help build lists that are right for you.

Go over all four of your lists one at a time, refine them, and make them as complete and accurate as you can. Every time you do that, you'll get a better understanding of where you are right now.

Sometimes it helps to get a global perspective of where you are.

THE WORLD AND YOU IN IT

Try to figure out where you are in the world in general. Look for the critical ingredients of success and the key factors of growth. Know where the barriers are. And know the leading economic and social indicators that will guide you and affect your outcomes.

Know who the leaders are and be able to describe them. Know who your competitors and role models are, and see if they're doing things that you could do just as well. Balance your skills against theirs and see if you're better, the same, or not quite at their skill level. Know how many people out there are just like you. See if you have what it takes to do what you want to do.

Know how you relate to the individuals you work with or to those who are a part of your personal life. Are you the head honcho or a secure member? Or are you a small fish in a big pond?

Size up your relationships with all the different groups of people you come in contact with, especially if those people are going to have a significant impact on your designs for the future.

You may find, in spite of your good intentions and sincere desire to change, that it's almost impossible to come up with new ideas about yourself or your world. If you have trouble seeing the person you want to be or the places you want to go, it may be because of conceptual blocks.

CONCEPTUAL BLOCKS

Conceptual blocks are mental barriers that keep you from seeing things as they really are. They come in all shapes and sizes.

PERCEPTUAL BLOCKS

Perceptual blocks keep you from seeing things that are right in front of you. They appear when you have so many things to think about that you can't sort out the ones that are really important for planning. You can't see the forest for the trees.

On the other hand, you may have broken down an element

into such small pieces that you can no longer see it in its proper context. Or you may have ignored what other people thought and interpreted the facts according to the way you saw them. If you did either of these, you probably eliminated several options that would otherwise have been available to you.

You might also be so saturated with information that you can hardly remember any of it. This can be demonstrated by a simple little exercise.

Take a sheet of paper, and without looking at a telephone, draw a picture of the dial with all the properly placed numbers and letters. If you're like most people who use the phone a lot, your mind is probably so crammed full of details that you can't remember what either the dial or the pushbuttons look like.

CULTURAL AND ENVIRONMENTAL BLOCKS

Cultural taboos can keep you from walking around naked even when your air-conditioner is busted. And that's probably not the only tradition or social custom that keeps you from adapting to the changing nature of your world or from coming up with a variety of ways of planning your future.

If there's a part of your world that you don't approve of because of the way you were brought up, then you'll probably fail to recognize it as either a threat or an opportunity for change.

EMOTIONAL BLOCKS

Planning involves risk-taking. If you have no appetite for chaos and are afraid of taking risks, then you're going to have a hard time moving into an uncharted future.

On the other hand, uncontrolled enthusiasm or excessive zeal can shoot you right over an assessment of the past and present. You'd be so excited you'd miss everything around you.

And if you can't separate reality from fantasy, you're going to have a hard time trying to figure out what to do in the days ahead.

INTELLECTUAL AND EXPRESSIVE BLOCKS

Sometimes you run into conditions you can't describe because you don't understand them. You don't have the facts you need, and you don't know where to get them. And sometimes, when you think you know what you're doing, you can't express your situation in a way that will allow you to change.

A lack of expression will keep you from developing well-defined strategies, just as a lack of understanding will limit the number of strategies that are available to you.

Conceptual blocks must be removed before you can do much planning for the future. You'll see how to do that as you go through the rest of this book.

SUMMARY

Start your planning efforts by separating the wheat from the chaff. Look at your capabilities as well as your limitations, and see what opportunities you have for making the changes you think are important.

Use analytic methods to examine your imaginative hunches. Remember that planning and poker have a lot in common. They both call for decisions that are based on incomplete and sometimes inaccurate information. To be good at either one, you have to know what you're holding, and you have to know everything you can about the rules and strategies of the game.

The next step in the planning process, after you've completed your investigation, is to take the information you have and decide what you're going to do with it.

DECISION

By now, you should have a pretty good idea of who you are and what kind of world you live in. After you refine and clarify that information, you'll be able to develop several different things you can do to be successful. And then you can choose the course of action that's best for you.

ALTERNATIVES AND CHOICES

One of the most effective ways of coming up with alternative courses of action is to brainstorm. Brainstorming is a problem-solving technique that deals with the free and spontaneous generation of ideas. You can use it here to develop plans for the future.

The first step in developing different courses of action is to understand the relationships that exist between your strengths, weaknesses, opportunities, and threats. Then you've got to develop those relationships so you're doing things that will generate success. You'll have a much better idea of what you're going to do after you combine your four lists as shown in Figure 5.

COMBINE THE GOOD

Look at Square 1 in Figure 5. It asks you to combine your list of strengths with your list of opportunities.

Put your two lists side by side. Then compare the things you're good at and like to do with what you think are good chances

FIGURE 5

RELATIONSHIPS BETWEEN STRENGTHS, WEAKNESSES, OPPORTUNITIES, AND THREATS

	OPPORTUNITIES	THREATS
STRENGTHS	1	2
WEAKNESSES	3	4

for success. Figure out which opportunities exist because of your strengths and which strengths exist only because of the opportunities that are available.

If you look at Figure 6, you'll see that some of the strengths and opportunities that were presented as examples in the last chapter have already been combined.

In the first example, an opportunity exists because there isn't much competition. The person also has a lot of customers and a good product line. Those opportunities have been combined with some of the person's strengths, like being a hard worker and doing a good job of selling things to other people. Besides those strengths, they also like to meet new people, call on customers, and close a sale.

That person should know by this time what the strategies of good salesmanship are. And they can probably come up with some ideas for capitalizing on that combination in the future. But one thing they may not know is the *effect* that this combination will have on their success.

Think of putting fuel in your gas tank. Up to now, you've been using regular gas, and that probably kept you moving at a steady pace. But if you could mix a high-octane fuel (strengths) with a supercharger (opportunities), you'd be off to the races.

Just knowing that you're going into a good situation with your best foot forward will give you a new sense of confidence that will propel you toward success. And your opportunities and strengths will always work together to your advantage if you recognize the relationship and then capitalize on it.

FIGURE 6

COMBINING OPPORTUNITIES AND STRENGTHS

OPPORTUNITY-A
1. Little or no competition
2. Lots of customers
3. Good product line
4. Ideal economic conditions

STRENGTHS
4. Selling products or ideas to other people
5. Willing to work hard
6. Meeting new people
9. Closing a sale
10. Calling on customers

OPPORTUNITY-B
5. Lots of friends
6. Membership in a business association

STRENGTHS
1. Speaking in public
2. Playing a musical instrument

OPPORTUNITY-C
7. Rapidly growing community
10. Strong family support

STRENGTH
7. Accept risk

(OTHER OPPORTUNITIES) ...

Figure 6 points out other ways of combining these two elements. If a person has lots of friends and belongs to a friendly group, they may be able to parlay their talents of speaking in public or playing a musical instrument.

If they're in a rapidly growing community, and if their family is behind them, they might be in a position to take a risk on a speculative venture.

As you go through this exercise of combining strengths and opportunities, consider every idea you come up with, no matter how farfetched it may seem when you first think of it. And write it down as soon as it comes to your mind.

Brainstorming will work for you if you can tear down your conceptual barriers and keep from jumping the gun on any idea. What you want most of all, is sudden and spontaneous insight, because that's going to produce the most ideas.

After you've come up with some general ideas, rewrite them as specific things to do in the future. Take one or two of the best ideas and think up as many ways of carrying them out as you can. Identify a few simple tasks that you can do right away. They'll give you a good start on the road to success.

Sometimes you'll come up with seat-of-the-pants ideas that'll be based on your experience in dealing with similar issues. Don't discount that intuitive ability, but at the same time, don't let your intuition overrule objective decision making.

COMBINE THE BAD

After you've compared your list of strengths with your list of opportunities, take a look at Square 4 of the diagram. It asks you to compare your list of weaknesses with your list of threats.

Look again at how the two lists relate to each other. See how some threats exist only because of your weaknesses, and how some weaknesses exist only because of threats you think are out there.

In this case, you want to keep from doing things you're not good at and don't like to do, especially in threatening situations that keep you from being successful.

Taking an example from Figure 7, you find that a person's

FIGURE 7

COMBINING THREATS AND WEAKNESSES

THREAT-A
   5. Shortage of available cash
   6. Lack of time
   8. High cost of education
   9. Limited opportunity for advancement

   WEAKNESS
   2. Taking examinations
   3. Concentrating on difficult tasks

THREAT-B
   10. Oppressive governmental regulations

   WEAKNESS
   7. Writing up sales reports
   10. Doing busy work

THREAT-C
   3. Number of dissatisfied customers

   WEAKNESSES
   1. Handling other people's complaints
   4. Controlling my temper
   5. Coping with physical or emotional stress
   9. Talking on the telephone

(OTHER THREATS) . . .

lack of advancement is due to their educational background. You also can see that at the present time, that person doesn't have the time or money to go back to school. Besides that, they know they have a hard time taking examinations and they find it hard to concentrate on difficult tasks.

Until that person can find the time and money to pay for their education, and until they can develop the skills that will get them through additional coursework, they'd better not try to go back to school.

If a person is having problems with customer complaints because of their short temper and inability to handle stress, then they'd better see if they can get transferred to another position or look for work elsewhere.

Compare items on your lists of weaknesses and threats that are similar to these. See where you can eliminate them, especially where they might be combined.

OTHER COMBINATIONS

Don't waste your time in Square 2, thinking of how you can match your list of strengths against your list of threats. And don't linger in Square 3, trying to exploit an opportunity by doing things you aren't good at or don't like to do. If you spend time in these areas, your opportunities will slip by, or you'll be overtaken by an outside threat.

Concentrate instead on using your strengths to exploit every opportunity you come in contact with. At the same time, stay away from combinations of weaknesses and threats. If you're successful at this, you should be able to spend 80 to 90 percent of your time doing what you want to do in situations that are are going to help you. On the other hand, you shouldn't spend more than 10 to 20 percent of your time trying to get through a threatening situation by doing something you don't enjoy doing or aren't very good at.

Go through this brainstorming process again and again, and fine-tune your thoughts until you can come up with several ideas that are right for you. They'll form the essence of your goals and objectives.

GOALS AND OBJECTIVES

A goal is a broad, idealistic statement of something you're

hoping to carry out. You usually don't have a specific time for completing a goal. And you don't go into a lot of detail on how you're going to do it. As an example, one of your goals may be to lose some weight sometime over the next few months.

An objective, on the other hand, is a clear, concise statement of an activity you want to complete by a certain date. When you develop an objective, you state exactly what you're going to do to reach your hoped-for accomplishment.

Objectives can almost always be measured in some way. Questions of how much, how far, how big, or how many can usually be answered. That makes it a lot easier to tell whether your objectives have been reached or not. An example of an objective would be your desire to lose seven pounds by the end of a three-week period.

Goals and objectives help you move from where you are to where you want to be. They aren't much use, however, unless they're flexible. That's because life is dynamic, fluctuating, and always changing. So you have to keep renewing your goals and objectives, or they'll soon be out of date and lose their importance.

Goals and objectives can be either positive or negative, and they can either drive you toward something or away from it. If your goal is to lose weight, you may want to look slimmer (positive) or avoid looking fat (negative).

Milestones are intermediate steps you carry out while you're on your way to meeting your objectives. If you space your milestones close together, you'll satisfy them in relatively short periods of time. That will boost your morale, give you a greater sense of accomplishment, and generate the enthusiasm you'll need to reach your over-all goals and objectives.

All your goals, objectives, and milestones should be based on realistic assumptions of what's coming up on the horizon.

PLANNING ASSUMPTIONS

Before you start developing your goals and objectives, you need to make some assumptions about what you think is going to happen over the next few months or years.

A planning assumption is a gut feeling you have that something is true and can be taken for granted. Planning assumptions are based on investigative findings that relate to you and the world you live in. These assumptions can involve anything you think will have an impact on your life, like economic conditions, anticipated business developments, or changes in your social life.

After you've established your planning assumptions, you can start developing your goals and objectives.

HOW TO DEVELOP GOALS AND OBJECTIVES

Here's a list of suggestions that will help you develop your short-term and long-range goals and objectives.

KNOW WHAT YOU'RE DOING

Take the ideas you developed while brainstorming and write down some hoped-for accomplishments. Clarify the intent of these initial goals by putting together some specific objectives that will help you reach them. The key task in this exercise is to identify the outcomes, achievements, or expected accomplishments you're going to shoot for.

KNOW WHERE YOU'RE GOING

Identify the major steps or milestones that have to be completed for you to meet your overall goals and objectives. Try to pinpoint the most likely dates when you think you'll reach your milestones and accomplish your objectives.

KNOW HOW YOU'RE GOING TO GET THERE

Make a list of the methods you're going to use and the resources you'll need to reach your goals and objectives. Try to identify other people who might help or interfere with your efforts.

KNOW IF YOU'VE DONE IT

Determine what measures you're going to use to figure out if and when you've really reached the end of your journey. These will be called your performance measures.

BE REALISTIC

Your goals and objectives should be realistic and attainable, and they should represent things you really want and are willing to work for. If it looks like you can't reach a goal, back off and establish a more realistic outcome. If a goal looks too easy, raise your sights a little higher.

In developing your goals, it's more important to choose the direction you want to go, instead of choosing a specific place where you want to end up. That's because the journey is more important than the destination, as you'll discover in later sections of this book.

GO FOR THE SHORT SHOT

In addition to your long-range goals, develop some short-term objectives that you can reach in the next three to six months. If you can get in the habit of reaching milestones or short-term objectives, you'll have a lot more success in reaching your long-range goals.

ESTABLISH YOUR CRITERIA

Your goals and objectives should be reasonable, specific, challenging, and measurable. They should be consistent with each other, and they should be connected to a reward system so you'll always be motivated to achieve them.

But even if you're highly motivated, mental barriers can keep you from seeing where you want to be in the future.

CONCEPTUAL BLOCKBUSTING

If you're having a hard time brainstorming new ideas for goals and objectives, you'll want to study these conceptual blockbusting techniques.

ASK QUESTIONS

Asking questions is an excellent way of freeing up your thoughts. As simple as that sounds, you might be afraid to do it, especially if somewhere back in elementary school you were laughed at because someone thought you were dumb.

The number of people who refuse to stop and ask directions when they're lost is enormous. And it always seems to include people who're coming for dinner.

MAKE LISTS

Making lists of things to do is another way of consciously breaking down thought barriers. Lists not only help your memory, they also let you see how different events can come together. List-making is even more productive when you're able to come up with several different ways of describing your tasks, because that can lead to different ways of completing them.

POSTPONE JUDGMENT

Postponing judgment of what is important and what is not, is one of the most effective ways of breaking down thought barriers. This allows your ideas to survive until they reach consciousness where you can deal with them without prejudice. Brainstorming, which was mentioned earlier, is one of the best techniques you can use to generate open and free ideas.

STIMULATE YOUR SENSES

You'll have a much easier time developing your goals and objectives if you use all five of your senses. This is especially true if you can think of all the steps you have to take to reach your goals. If you have these steps in your mind's eye, you'll have a much better chance of completing them.

Sensory stimulation is a very effective way of breaking down conceptual barriers, especially those that block your memory. It's easy to remember a fall football game if you can smell the grass on the playing field, see the brightly colored leaves, taste hot dogs and coffee, and hear the sounds of the crowd and the marching band.

Your ability to recall stimuli is limited only by your imagination. So approach your goals and objectives with all of your senses. Taste them, smell them, see them, hear them, and touch them if you can. You'll have a much easier time figuring out where you're going if you can get a vivid image of what you're trying to do.

Once you have your goals and objectives firmly in mind, the next step is to write them down.

HOW TO WRITE YOUR GOALS AND OBJECTIVES

Your goals and objectives should always be written down so you know exactly what you're supposed to do. Here are some tips that will help you in your efforts.

WRITE RIGHT

Avoid exaggerations, misconceptions, idealistic terms, oversimplifications, opinions subject to change, understated or overstated words, and terms that have a wide range of meaning. Use precise terms so there's never a question of what you're doing. That's the only way you'll know whether or not you've been successful.

BE SPECIFIC

Try to be as specific as possible without being too restrictive. Designate a certain number of pounds, don't just say you want to lose weight. If you're planning to reach a professional goal, spell it out so you know exactly what you're shooting for. As long as you remain flexible in your planning, you'll be able to change your goals whenever you feel it's necessary.

SUMMARY

Develop your goals and objectives as soon as you've got a good handle on who you are and what kind of world you live in. But before you write them down, demolish the thought barriers that keep you from freely expressing where you want to go and what you want to do.

Once you've decided on your future course of action, you have to organize your efforts to carry it out. That's what you'll learn to do in the next chapter.

ORGANIZATION

This chapter contains several suggestions that will help you organize your planning efforts. The first suggestion will help you find out how important your tasks are.

PRIORITIES

If you're like most people, you probably spend 80 to 90 percent of your time doing things that aren't important and hardly ever get you anywhere. Planning will help you turn that around and get you where you want to go.

GUIDELINES

Edwin Bliss, in his book *Getting Things Done: The ABCs of Time Management*, provides some excellent guidelines for evaluating tasks and establishing priorities. Here are the categories he uses.
  1. **Important and Urgent.** These tasks belong at the top of your list. You've got to do them right away or you'll have all hell to pay.
  2. **Important But Not Urgent.** These tasks should be near the top. But lots of people ignore them because they can be

postponed. They include things like getting a physical exam, writing a letter to a friend, or saying, "I love you."
3. **Urgent But Not Important**. These tasks tend to be high on other people's lists. If you put them ahead of the tasks you think are important, you're probably looking for approval from others.
4. **Busy Work**. These tasks can provide a welcome relief if you control them. But you'll never reach your goals and objectives if you spend too much on busy work.
5. **Wasted Time**. Don't even think about wasting time.

PROBLEMS WITH URGENCY

The basic principle behind planning is to give highest priority to important tasks.

People who set priorities according to urgency are probably responding to short-term crises. They spend so much time putting out fires that they never get to work on the things that are really important to them. They put off important things until they think the time is ripe. But then, before they know it, their time is up and they have to drop everything to take care of another urgent task that has to be done right away.

With little time remaining, they scramble to complete their task. Then, when they're almost done, they discover a better solution. But it's too late to start over, so they wind up with a lousy performance. They wish they could've done things differently, but there's no time to change because another crisis has worked its way to the top as the cycle continues.

Urgency is a legitimate concern, but you'll be much better off if you can set priorities in terms of importance. Obviously, if something is both important *and* urgent it should get top priority.

ASSIGNING PRIORITIES

Go through your list of things to do and ask yourself if each task is moving you closer to your lifetime goals, or if it's sending you off in a different direction. If the task is directly related to your goals, put a star by it. If it's not, then figure out some way to get rid of it, give it to someone else, or put it on the bottom of the pile.

Arrange your list of starred items in order of importance. Then start your day by doing the things that give you the most pleasure and provide the biggest payoff.

Sometimes it makes sense to work on a task that's not as urgent or important as another. If it doesn't take much time, and if the benefits are substantial, then go ahead and do it. It will serve as a warm-up exercise and will help build momentum for more important tasks.

Say, for example, that your most important task is something that could take all day. You may have other tasks, like phone calls to make or assignments to delegate, that aren't as important but are best done early in the day. Get those less important tasks out of the way first, and you'll have clear sailing the rest of the day for your major task.

Assign your priorities first thing in the morning or the last thing the night before. Your day will be much more productive if you do it that way instead of stopping to establish priorities every time you're ready to begin a new task. You'll be happier and more relaxed, because you'll be in control of your time and you'll know that important things are being tended to.

Reexamine your priorities from time to time so you always know what comes first. Feel free to change priorities after you start working on your plan if you have a good reason for doing so. And don't be afraid to say "no" to unimportant tasks that can disrupt your overall strategy.

Just make sure your priorities are realistic and well-suited to what you're trying to do. When you're standing knee-deep in alligators, it's hard to remember that you were supposed to clean the swamp.

Knowing what you're going to do is only one part of planning. It's just as important to know how well you did it.

PERFORMANCE MEASURES

Everyone seems to ask these two questions when they're involved in planning. "How do I know if I'm headed in the right direction?" and "How can I tell if I'm successful?"

Sometimes it's easy to see what you've done. You lose 15 pounds or you don't. You save $1500 or you don't. You get your promotion or you don't. These objectives are fairly easy to measure.

But it's not so easy to know if you're on the right track if you don't have some way of measuring your performance. So *before* you start out you should know what measures you're going to use and how you're going to use them.

Here are some yardsticks you can use to measure your performance.

1. Your strengths and weaknesses.
2. Your previous history of success and failure.
3. Levels of achievement you think are possible.
4. Expectations of people you think are evaluating you, and your feelings of how important their expectations really are.
5. Actual progress toward the goals and objectives you expect to reach, as measured by facts and figures.
6. What it costs you in time and other resources to reach your goals and objectives.

The best measure of success is your self-image, which is the set of values you hold for yourself. This *ideal self* is greatly influenced by social factors. It tends to reflect the status you have among groups and individuals that are important to you.

Different people see things in different ways, so it's up to you to know who's going to decide whether you've reached your goals and objectives or not. If somebody other than you is going to evaluate your progress, it should be a group or an individual whose opinions you respect and are willing to abide by. Any other assessments, whether good or bad, will contribute little or nothing to the development of your future goals.

Say, for example, that you're a salesman. You're now selling $750,000 worth of goods, and your goal is to increase that to $1,000,000. What are your measures of success? The number of dollars? How about your relationships with customers, co-workers, and members of your family? How will they measure your success? What will you have to sacrifice in terms of personal relationships to reach your financial goal?

Questions like these point out the need to identify performance measures before you start off on your plan. And even then, you may wonder if you've ever reached your goal or not.

HAVE YOU ARRIVED?

There are no *endings* in life except one. So one of the most important things you can learn when making plans is to give up the concept of endings. If you don't, your quest for a simple, happy ending will eventually cause frustration.

That sounds pessimistic, but only if you think life is very simple. It's not, it's very complex. That's why it's fun.

To get the most out of life, you need to think about it as a long, never-ending pathway that stretches out ahead of you, with many other pathways leading off to either side. The pathways you choose will be determined by your goals and objectives and the success you have in carrying out your plans.

You'll probably never *arrive*, because all of your really important tasks will never be finished. There may be an occasional break in the action, but as you get close to reaching one goal, another one that's going to be more important will spring up ahead of you.

Each new goal will bring with it the challenge and excitement of a chase. That's what makes life fun and keeps you growing. Just think of how god-awful life would be if there were no challenges, no stars to shoot for, or no dreams of things to come.

There's no guarantee that planning will satisfy all your desires. As a matter-of-fact, there's a lot of risk involved in planning.

THE ELEMENT OF RISK

Before you develop a plan of action, you should know something about the element of risk that's involved. You especially need to know how much risk you can afford and still be happy with what you're doing.

Look at the key events in your plan. They're the ones on which you're going to base your best estimate of what lies ahead. Then figure out what your odds are for successfully completing those events.

Say, for example, that you have to complete five separate events for your plan to be successful. And you figure the chance of success for each event to be 80 percent.

It may surprise you to know that your chance of success for all five events taken together is not 80 percent, but 33 percent. You'd only have one chance in three for your whole plan to be successful when the chance of success for each of your five events is 80 percent.

To figure out your chance of success for a plan made up of several events, you multiply the odds of the first event by the odds of the second event by the odds of the third event, on down the line. In this case, multiplying 80 percent by itself five times turns out to be 33 percent.

If your plan is made up of lots of events, the odds for each of them being successful must be extraordinarily high if you don't want your whole plan to collapse over just one of them. In order to increase the probability of your five-event plan to 90 percent, you'd have to increase the probability of success for each event to 98 percent.

It's obvious from this example that a simple plan, where only a few things can go wrong, will have a much better chance of being successful than one with several independent events.

The chances of success are important to know when you're trying to develop a plan. And no matter what the odds are, they're still a lot better when you plan than they would be if you cast your lot to the winds and hoped for the best.

SUMMARY

Decide what parts of your plan are really important and set out to do those first. Organize your tasks according to a timetable so you can get a better idea of what you have to do. Figure out ways of measuring your performance so you'll be able to see how well you've done. And be sure you know what the odds are for your being successful.

There's one more step to take to before you actually start planning. You have to prepare yourself for what lies ahead. The next chapter will tell you how to do that.

PREPARATION

Planning gets into high gear when you decide where you want to go. In this chapter, you'll find out what you need to know about getting ready to take that journey. You'll learn about good and bad planning, and you'll discover ways to ensure a successful outcome.
Now that you're in the starting blocks and have come to your mark, it's time to get physically and emotionally set to go.

GET SET TO GO

The amount of detail you put into your plan should be balanced by the amount of experience you have in planning. If you don't have a lot of experience (and even if you do) there are several things you'll want to watch out for as you fine-tune your efforts.

BE PSYCHOLOGICALLY READY

Believe in what you're doing, and commit your time and energy to making the changes you really think are necessary. Make up your mind, as you build your plan, that you're going to stick with it. Convince yourself that it's what you really want to do and that you're capable of carrying it out.

Understand the concepts behind your plan and the principles that support it. Be realistic about your projections and know what's expected of you.

MAKE A COMMITMENT

You'll be more likely to follow through with your plan if you commit yourself to doing it. And you'll have a better chance of keeping that commitment if you share it with someone you trust and respect. That person can, in return, help you determine your strengths and weaknesses, assess your progress, and evaluate your results.

PLAY THE ODDS

Planning is effected by chance. Sometimes your plans will work out and sometimes they won't. There are no sure bets, and any plans you make for the future have to deal with uncertainty. You can, however, save yourself a lot of grief if you know what your chances for success are before you start.

Once you know what your odds are, do everything you can to improve them. Concentrate on events where you have a good chance of succeeding. Avoid areas where success is almost impossible. Change your strategy wherever you can if it will help improve your odds. If you work at planning long enough, you'll increase your odds to where success will almost be inevitable.

DEVELOP THE PLANNING HABIT

Get in the habit of planning everything you do. If you have a number of errands to do, make a list and take care of them in the order that makes the most sense. Figure out which one should be done first and which ones can be done at the same time. Know which errands have to be completed before others can begin.

Think through your schedules. Write down each task and ask yourself how long it'll take you to do it. Keep doing this until planning becomes automatic.

FIND A PLACE

For every action, there is an equal and opposite reaction. It's the same with planning. Hostility, indifference, and imaginary delays can bombard your planning efforts from all directions.

Your physical surroundings and the people around you should contribute to your efforts, not frustrate them. So to keep from getting sidetracked, find a place where you'll be encouraged to plan.

Experiment with different settings. Work alone or with someone. Ask for suggestions, or keep to yourself. See what works best for you and stick with it. Stay away from settings where it's hard for you to succeed.

STAY IN CONTROL

Develop lots of day-to-day objectives where you have a good chance of being successful. You'll have more control over them than you will over great big goals that span a lifetime. And the more control you have, the more success you'll have in the future.

Build on the success of your short-term objectives and incorporate that into your long-range plans whenever you can. Then things will start turning around. As you find more and more success, you'll develop more and more control over the whole planning process.

IDENTIFY YOUR MILESTONES

Write down all the steps you're going to take along the way. And then keep your overall plan in your mind's eye as you go through your day-to-day activities. If you have your plan laid out clearly in front of you, you'll know where you've been, where you are, and where you're headed.

Streamline your plan so it's easy to follow. Avoid overlap, conflict, and duplication. And be sure to have a contingency plan ready in case something goes wrong.

Break up your planning schedule so everything doesn't happen all at once. You can do that by scheduling activities and events that cover different time spans, like a day, a week, a year, or five years. When things are happening all the time, your enthusiasm is bound to be high.

PREPARE YOUR RESOURCES

Get your resources in place before you start so you don't have to fumble around trying to find them when they're needed. This applies to obvious resources like money, personnel, and supplies. But it also relates to things like space and time. And be sure to use your resources where they'll have the greatest impact. Don't let anything go to waste.

KNOW YOUR OPTIONS

Identify every course of action that's available to you. Weigh the advantages and disadvantages of each of them and then figure out which one promises to be the most successful in accomplishing your goals and objectives.

Translate your chosen course of action into a concise statement of what you're going to do, and when, where, and how you're going to do it. If anyone should ask what you're up to, you should be able to respond in one clearly thought-out sentence.

KNOW WHEN TO STOP

Don't get so wrapped up in the process of planning that you fail to recognize when it's time to stop planning and start moving.

And after you're on your way, be sure you know when it's time to stop and make adjustments or start a new plan.

KEEP BRAINSTORMING

Keep analyzing the interaction between your strengths and weaknesses and the opportunities and threats that exist in your environment. Don't let up, even when you start reaching your goals and objectives. As long as you're flexible and keep thinking about what you want to do, you'll be able to come up with alternative courses of action whenever it looks like changes in strategy might be helpful.

Brainstorming works best when several people are involved.

So get together with people who are close to you and willing to help. Use their input to clarify your strengths and weaknesses and to identify opportunities and threats.

As you zero in on your goals and objectives, you should be aware of the difference between good and bad planning.

WHAT MAKES GOOD PLANNING

Good planning isn't always successful. That's because there are just too many variables that can apply. On the other hand, poor planning doesn't always fail. That's because planning of any kind is still better than no planning at all.

If you want to be successful, you should follow the standards on which good planning is based. Here are the most important ones.

ACCURACY

Your plans must be based on concrete facts and real situations. So you have to be very accurate when you describe the way things are and the way you'd like them to be. The information you gather about yourself and the world around you must be the best available. And your plan must contain a clear picture of what you think is going to happen, including a realistic estimate of your chances for success.

VISION

You have to be able to see new opportunities and take advantage of them. You have to anticipate obstacles and come up with effective ways of getting rid of them. You have to have alternate plans even before you need them. Your success in planning will depend on your ability to see what's happening to you and to use what you find whenever and wherever you can.

SIMPLICITY

Your plan should be simple, well organized, and clearly understood. Tasks and activities should be spelled out. Realistic timetables should be set. And you should have a good idea of what you need in the way of resources. Just remember that a simple plan is much easier for you to carry out than one that's complicated and hard to follow.

COMPETENCE

Planning cannot be left to chance. You should have, or be ready to get, the personal expertise and discipline you need to be successful in carrying out your plan. If you don't have the necessary skills, you should take immediate steps toward making yourself a competent planner. Practice and further study are the two most effective things you can do to build your planning competence.

FLEXIBILITY

You should be responsive to everything that can possibly happen to you. If your plan is unworkable or obsolete, you should be flexible enough to modify, change, or revise it as needed. If either you or your plan is inflexible to change, the resulting stress can be functionally and psychologically disastrous. Your plan can collapse and so can you.

Even if your plan is a good one, you've got to have what it takes to carry it out.

HOW TO BE A GOOD PLANNER

There are two ways you can tell if your planning has been successful. The first is to see if you reached your ultimate goal. The second is to see if what you gained from your planning effort was worth the time, effort and other resources that went into it.
To be a better planner than you already are, you should make sure you have as many of the following characteristics as you can.

CHARACTERISTICS OF GOOD PLANNERS

Here are some characteristics that are generally found in people who are successful planners. Compare this list with what you already know about yourself.

Inquisitive. Good planners spend time trying to figure out why things are as they seem to be.

Creative. Good planners look for new ideas or new ways of applying old ones.

Competitive. Good planners enjoy intellectual competition and are skilled at verbal give-and-take. They like to test other people's positions and look for strengths and weaknesses in other people's ideas.

Practical. Good planners don't try to kid themselves about what can be done, how fast it can be completed, and what resources are needed. They're realistic, enthusiastic, and very pragmatic.

Confident. Good planners are able to cope with criticism and rejection. Logic and reason help them persevere no matter what the odds are.

Informed. Good planners keep up with developments in other fields.

There are noticeable differences between people who are good planners and those who are not.

THE DIFFERENCE BETWEEN PLANNERS

After some people develop a plan they commit themselves so firmly to it that they resist all distractions and do everything they can to accomplish their intended goal.

Other people can't stick to a plan, no matter how well it's spelled out. They give up easily when faced with even the slightest obstacle or distraction.

This difference isn't hard to understand. People differ in their capacity to develop and carry out plans just as they differ in their capacity to solve intellectual problems or perform acts of skill.

If you can recognize this difference, it'll keep you from getting discouraged when you run into difficulties. Just do the best you can and try to get better at what you're doing.

Planning is still the best way to approach the future. The secret of successful planning is to make sure your plan is simple, easy to understand, and comfortable to work with. If it is, you'll be able to move forward with determination and honest effort.

If you make mistakes, or if your plan doesn't work out like you think it should, you can still get back on track. But things will go a lot easier for you if you know how to stay out of trouble in the first place.

CAUSES OF FAILURE AND HOW TO AVOID THEM

Here are some of the causes of planning failures, along with ways of avoiding them.

EXCESSIVE OPTIMISM

People who are overly optimistic or all fired up to succeed usually fail to recognize potential problems as they develop. They discard bad news and hear only what they want to hear. When serious problems come up, their lack of foresight keeps them from making necessary adjustments. That's when their plans start to fall apart.

You can avoid the dangers of excessive optimism by staying within the framework of the inside-out model that's been highlighted throughout this book. A thorough analysis of strengths, weaknesses, threats, and opportunities will temper your optimism with reality.

LACK OF COMPETENT ADVICE

Planning efforts usually fail when people insulate themselves from the advice, suggestions, and counsel of others. Nobody can hope to know and understand every factor that might affect them in the future. And those who think otherwise are inviting failure.

The use of brainstorming techniques, as suggested in the planning model, will stimulate others into sharing their ideas for success. As long as you take their advice openly and examine it carefully, you'll go a long way toward insuring the success of any planning effort you undertake.

INABILITY TO RECOGNIZE CHANGE

Sometimes people get so locked up in their plans and lists of things to do, that they fail to see the changes that are happening in the world around them. When they finally recognize that conditions are no longer the way they were at the beginning, it's usually too late to shift gears. Their plans quickly become a casualty of their shortsightedness.

Continuous review of your progress, together with an ongoing assessment of outside influences, will help you see changes when they occur. If you can make a habit of investigating and analyzing the things that happen to you, you'll be able to see much farther ahead, and you'll anticipate changes before they occur.

DOING AS YOU DAMN WELL PLEASE

Stubbornness in the face of conflicting evidence almost always guarantees failure. This trait is frequently found in people who are only involved in planning because they have to be. If they feel they've been coerced into planning against their will, then their stubbornness is probably serving as a way of expressing their dissatisfaction.

You can't hope to succeed if you deliberately set out to fail as a way of making a point. You've got to believe in the promise that planning holds for the future. If you do, and if you can replace your stubbornness with flexibility, you'll not only feel better, but you'll also have a better chance of getting things done.

LACK OF BALANCED GROWTH

Some people find immediate success in planning. That can cause problems later if they limit their efforts to just those areas where they've been successful and deliberately avoid working in other areas. Their overall growth will eventually slow down and then stop altogether.

To ensure balanced growth, you need to make a thorough and accurate assessment of all your strengths and weaknesses. Then you need to develop plans for change wherever change is warranted, regardless of the probability of success. As you discover successful planning techniques, transfer them to areas where you're having problems.

When planning gets to be habit-forming, you'll automatically start using your planning skills in every area that needs change.

FAILURE TO MONITOR RESULTS

People usually make a shambles of their planning efforts when they ignore performance measures and fail to analyze their results. They have no way of knowing what's going on because they haven't paid any attention to their milestones. When they don't evaluate their problems against previously determined benchmarks, their mistakes go unnoticed, and then their whole plan breaks down.

To prevent this kind of disaster, you should always evaluate your progress against standards that have already been set up. Build on your successes and take steps to keep from repeating your mistakes. Just be sure that when you establish your performance measures, you build in ways of checking to see if you met them or not.

FEAR OF THE UNKNOWN

Planning activities can also turn out badly when people are afraid of failure or have a fear of the unknown. If they're afraid of taking chances and hesitate to move forward when the opportunity presents itself, they'll stagnate, and their plans will break down completely.

You can conquer fear by using the strategy Dale Carnegie

outlined in his book, ***How To Stop Worrying And Start Living***. Here are his suggestions.
1. Ask yourself what's the worst that can possibly happen.
2. Write down precisely what you're worrying about.
3. Prepare to accept the worst if you have to.
4. Write down as many solutions to your problem as you can think of.
5. Decide on the best solution.
6. Start immediately to carry out that decision.
7. Calmly proceed to improve on what you see as the worst.

Don't isolate yourself from planning failures. Plan instead to deal with them head-on as contingencies.

PLANNING FOR CONTINGENCIES

A contingency is something you think might happen. But when it does, it usually comes when you least expect it. It's like an emergency, and it's usually related to whatever it is you're working on. Contingencies can be devastating. But if you plan for them, you can either avoid them or get through them without any trouble.

One good thing about having a contingency plan is that its very existence, and the approach it implies, will help guarantee that you'll never need it.

People who have very detailed and complicated plans tend to display a lot of inertia and irrationality when contingencies come up. That's because their rigid plans, with no provision for contingencies, can't allow for spontaneous responses when an inevitable surprise occurs.

Sometimes contingencies can help you, especially if you're able to come up with creative solutions to the problems they create. The demands these spontaneous outbursts put on you can enrich your understanding of the planning process and increase your chances for a successful outcome.

Speaking of chances, you should know the effect that luck can have on your planning activities.

LUCK AND PLANNING

Luck is the effect that chance has on your life. You can improve your luck by being prepared for good fortune whenever you run into it. You just have to recognize it when it happens and apply yourself to the opportunity it presents.

It's easy to capitalize on chance and improve your luck if you've done a good job of identifying the strengths, interests, and personal characteristics you'd like to develop. All you have to do is demonstrate your positive qualities whenever you get an opportunity to do so.

The process is fairly simple. The more you know about what you really want, the better you'll be at applying yourself when a chance comes up. And the more chances you have, the more good luck you'll be able to get out of them. The key lies in being able to apply your strengths whenever you get a chance to do it.

If you waste your time trying to reach unreasonable goals, your frustration will keep you from seeing chances that are right in front of you. And the psychological insecurity that comes with frustration will keep you from responding successfully no matter how many chances you get.

SUMMARY

Be physically and emotionally ready to set your plan in motion. Know what makes a good plan and a good planner. Recognize some of the probable causes of failure and know how to avoid them. Plan for the problems you hope will never come. And whenever opportunity knocks, be sure you're there to answer the door.

Now you're ready for action. In the next chapter you'll discover eighteen separate suggestions that will help you put your plan in operation.

IMPLEMENTATION

Now that you know what you want to do, it's time to start doing it. But since your plan can't run on its own, you're going to have to stay on top of it to make sure it takes you where you want to go.

MAKING IT WORK

Here are eighteen suggestions you can use to make sure your plan runs smoothly.

1. START WHEN READY

Start working on your plan as soon as you have everything you need. The worst thing you can do is sit in the starting blocks and procrastinate. Don't worry about contingencies. If you've planned for them, you can handle them as they come up. If you find out later that you've made a mistake, admit it, back up, and start over.

Your starting time is important if you're going to get people's attention and gain an early response. But it's not always easy to tell when that should be. Sometimes you get an instinctive feeling of when you should get started. You either feel dissatisfied with your present position, or the amount of pressure you're under tells you that the time is ripe.

Your starting position should be set wherever you can see potential payoffs coming quickly and clearly.

2. LAUNCH A LEADING TASK

Your initial effort should get you off dead center, break the bonds of inertia, and lead right into the rest of your plan. If it's going to take a tremendous amount of energy for you to get started, you probably want to make sure that the first task is an easy one.

3. DELEGATE

Know what you're going to do and what you can expect from others. Spend your time and energy on the most important tasks. Then delegate clear responsibility and authority for remaining tasks to people you can trust. Make sure they know what you're doing and are willing to help you reach your goals and objectives.

Once you've delegated full responsibility, give crystal-clear instructions and then back off and let the other people do the best they can. You'll be free to go to work on the things you do best and are most efficient at. As others complete their assignments, you can gather their results together with yours into a final product.

4. BE GOAL ORIENTED

Focus on your goals and objectives and move briskly toward their completion. Take shortcuts when you see them, and pass over any unnecessary tasks that get in your way. Running in place is a good way to work up a sweat, but it won't get you anywhere. So think about getting things done, not just doing things.

5. SEE WHAT YOU'RE DOING

You can do anything faster and better if you can see yourself getting it done. The key lies in the intensity of your vision and the depth of your concentration. The picture you form in your mind's eye will motivate you to complete your task.

It's a lot easier to see what you're doing if you can get rid of overblown standards and unreasonable expectations. Think instead of goals and objectives you know you can accomplish.

6. PLAY YOUR OWN GAME

You should be proactive, not reactive. Innovate wherever you can. Do your own thing and don't just follow the crowd. Concentrate on your long-term goals and accept short-term accomplishments as you reach them. Establish a climate that's conducive to change.

Your deadlines should be precise but flexible. Overly ambitious deadlines can inspire you to greater efforts or cause you to take short cuts. Easy deadlines can lead to procrastination. Indefinite deadlines are easily ignored and can cause your plan to collapse.

Accept as much risk as you can afford. The reason many people fill their days with unimportant, low priority work is because they don't want to face any more risk than they absolutely have to. They avoid the challenges of planning because they're afraid of things they can't see. Busywork keeps them occupied as a low risk, nonthreatening way of wasting time. Don't fall into the same trap.

7. WORK AT IT

Be willing to work. The only time you'll find success coming before work is in the dictionary.

Concentrate on what you're doing. Find some uninterrupted time and work on the really tough tasks. Prune back unnecessary tasks that slow you down and turn you away from your overall goal. Know your peak periods and use them to get things done. Save routine work for slow or secondary periods. If you can keep up a consistent level of effort, you'll make steady progress toward completion of your goals and objectives.

8. STUDY YOUR PLAN

Every time you reach a milestone, take time to figure out

where you are, what you've done to get there, and what you have to do to keep moving. Write down any unexpected events you run into along the way. Figure out what strategies work the best and come back to them whenever your progress is slowed or blocked. If you can gather a storehouse of information about where you've been, you'll be in much better control of your future.

9. CHECK YOUR PROGRESS

Keep track of where you're going as well as where you've been. Take time to reflect at the end of each day. Look at your list of tasks and see how well you did. The more you learn about the planning process, the easier it will be to carry it out in the future.

Incorporate your insights of today into your plans for tomorrow. Change unproductive patterns. You probably do 80 percent of your productive work in 20 percent of the time available, so make adjustments wherever they're needed.

Fill in extra time with special tasks. Spread your tasks over a longer period if you're short on time. Try to do better each day. Build a sense of improvement into your expectations.

10. STAY FLEXIBLE

Every well-drawn plan will be out of date by the time you put it in use. That's because everything around you is constantly changing. The only plan that can possibly be 100 percent up-to-date is one that's already full of mistakes.

You've got to know how you'll be affected by the success or failure of your plan. If you expect change, know how much change you're willing and able to take.

Diversity is the best protection against catastrophe. So try to figure out where problems are and anticipate when they're going to happen. Know when things are getting out of hand. Keep some alternative strategies ready in case your first plan doesn't work out. Replace strategies that fail to live up to your expectations.

Any changes you make in your plan will have to be in tune with your overall goals and objectives. That's why it's important to create a mental image of the revised version of your plan before you start on it.

Maintain a balanced outlook. Don't overreact or take too long. Keep faith with your plan. Don't give up on the whole thing if something goes wrong. Modify it, but stick with it. Compare your plan with those of the National Aeronautics and Space Administration (NASA). They never seem to give up. And ultimately they shot for the moon and made it.

11. KNOW YOUR TIME CONSTRAINTS

Develop a feel for how much you can do in a specified period of time. Parkinson's Law says work will expand to fill the time available for its completion. On the other hand, you can probably get rid of a lot of useless activity and wasted effort if you make less time available for what you have to do.

Know your deadlines. Maintain a tight schedule that keeps you from dawdling and procrastinating. Complete little tasks by using bits and pieces of time wherever you find them.

Set aside prime time for the really important tasks. Then consolidate your efforts in the time you have left and watch your productivity go up.

Keep track of the time you use. Manage time like money. You balance your checkbook to keep from being overdrawn, you should do the same with your calendar.

12. BE HONEST

If you find yourself faced with an impossible task, admit defeat and get rid of it. You'll just build up a lot of anxiety and frustration if you keep pushing against a stone wall. Come to terms with your tasks and be honest with yourself. Stick with your plan as long as you can, and try for simple solutions wherever possible. But bail out if you run into a dead end.

Remember your list of priorities, and don't get caught in the trap of overestimating the importance of what you're doing.

13. PLAN FOR GRADUAL IMPROVEMENT

Don't take spectacular leaps unless you're a trapeze artist. Look around you. There are few events in nature that happen all at once. They happen in bits and pieces over time, like the flowering of a rose or the growing of a tree. Recognize and use the power of patience.

14. KEEP MOTIVATED

The more you understand what you have to do, the more motivated you'll be to do it. Focus your attention on activities that you like, that are important to you, and that you think are worthwhile.

Give yourself a positive reward for reaching each one of your milestones. The rewards don't have to be expensive or lavish, just something you enjoy and look forward to having when you get where you want to go. If they're meaningful, they'll motivate you to do your best.

Include a system of rewards as part of your plan. But remember to give yourself a reward only when you earn it. And when you earn it, be sure you take it.

15. BE HAPPY

The way you feel about what you have to do will greatly affect the way you do it. If you're happy, you'll get done sooner and have fewer problems. On the other hand, if you're angry or dissatisfied, your work will drag on and you'll make a ton of mistakes.

You can't look forward to a hopeless future and expect to get anywhere. You have to think positively of things to come and of the rewards your efforts will bring you.

16. BE INTENSE

Work hard at being really good in at least one area of your life and then take pride in your accomplishment. If you pick one area and excel in it, your success will carry over into every other area you're involved in.

17. BE CONSISTENT

Try to succeed in every activity your plan calls for, no matter how important it is. Success is habit forming. If you can get in the habit of being successful, you'll make tremendous progress, and you'll be in a better position to handle any problems that might come up.

18. CONTINUE TO GROW

After you've mastered these simple procedures of inside-out planning, move on to other rational, systematic decisionmaking models. Be sure to choose one that involves a general analysis of where you are, the development of alternatives, and the implementation of a series of tasks. Just make sure the focus is on you and what you're able to do and not on some outside conditions over which you have no control.

SUMMARY

Pay close attention to the strategies that help get your plan underway. Make sure your planning principles are adhered to. And keep yourself in the right frame of mind as you carry out your plan.

You've designed your hoped-for future, and you've developed the steps needed to get you there. Now all you have to do is carry out your plan. If you do everything that's suggested in this book, and broaden your knowledge wherever you can, your planning efforts should all be successful.

A FINAL WORD

When asked why he spent so much time in planning and thinking about the future, Charles Kettering said, "My interest is in the future because I'm going to spend the rest of my life there."

Your future is now. Today is the first day of the rest of your life. By tomorrow, you'll have already lost part of it. And unlike so many other things, when you lose time, it's gone forever.

There are two ways you can go. You can lay back and take life as it comes to you. Or you can recognize the power in planning and take the time to decide what you really want.

If you leave everything to chance, you'll have about as much control of your destiny as a leaf in a hurricane. But if you try to intercept chance and take advantage of all that life has to offer, you'll live a happy, self-fulfilling life.

You discovered the steps involved in planning as you read through this book. They're simple and easy to follow. You can use them for something as big and impressive as designing a space program, or as simple as running through a day's errands.

Have the courage to start planning right now, even if you think it's a big step to take. You can't cross a chasm with lots of little jumps, and planning won't get any easier if you wait. Take this book along with you on your journey, and consult it like a friend.

Go for it. Do it now, cuz time's a wasting.

On your mark...Get set...GO!

BIBLIOGRAPHY

Adams, James L. *Conceptual Blockbusting*. San Francisco: San Francisco Book Co., Inc., 1976.

Bliss, Edwin C. *Getting Things Done: The ABC's of Time Management*, New York: Bantam Books, Inc., 1976.

Campbell, David. *If You Don't Know Where You're Going, You'll Probably End Up Somewhere Else*. Allen, Texas: Argus Communications, 1974.

Cargegie, Dale. *How to Stop Worrying and Start Living*. New York: Simon and Schuster, 1948.

Carr, A. H. Z. *How to Attract Good Luck*. New York: Cornerstone Library, 1952.

Dodgson, C. L. *The Complete Works of Lewis Carroll* (Pseud.) New York: Modern Library, Inc. 1936.

Ellis, Darryl. *Planning for Nonplanners: Planning Basics for Managers*. New York: American Management Association, 1980.

Ewing, David W. *The Human Side of Planning: Tool or Tyrant*. London: The Macmillan Company, 1969.

Sherman, James R. *REJECTION*. Golden Valley, Minnesota: Pathway Books, 1982.

INDEX

accuracy in planning: 45
advice, lack of competent: 48-49
Alice in Wonderland: 1
analytical planning: 3
assumptions, planning: 27-28
attitudes against planning: 8

benefits of planning: 5-6
Bliss, Edwin: 33
blockbusting, conceptual: 30-31
blocks, conceptual: 18-20
    perceptual: 18-19
    cultural and environmental: 19
    emotional: 19
    intellectual and expressive: 20
brainstorming: 21, 44-45

Carnegie, Dale: 50
change, inability to recognize: 49
combinations:
    strengths and
        opportunities: 21-33
    weaknesses and threats: 23-36
    others to avoid: 26
commitment: 4, 42
competency in planning: 46
conceptual blockbusting: 30-31
conceptual blocks: 18-20
consistency: 59

contingencies, planning for: 51
control of planning: 43
cultural and environmental
    blocks: 19
comparison of strengths and
    weaknesses: 13-14

dangers in planning: 6-7
deadlines, flexible: 55
definition of planning: 2-3
delegation: 54
Disney, Walt: 5
diversity: 56

emotional blocks: 19
endings: 37
environment, planning: 42-43
excessive optimism: 48

failure, causes of: 48-51
failure to monitor results: 50
fear of failure: 50
fear of the unknowwn: 9, 50
flexibility: 46, 56-57
flexible deadlines: 55
follow the leader planning: 3
Ford, Henry: 5
frustration: 1

goal orientation: 54
goals, defined: 26-27
goals and objectives: 2
   definition: 26-27
   developing: 28-29
   criteria for: 29
   writing: 31-32
good planning: 45-46
good planners: 46-47
gradual improvement: 58
growth, lack of: 6-7, 49-50

habit of planning: 42
happiness: 58
history of successes and
   failures: 15
honesty: 57

implementation: 5
inability to recognize change: 49
inside-out model: 9
insight: 23
intellectual and expressive
   blocks: 20
intensity: 58-59
intuition: 23
investigation: 4

judgment, postponing: 30

Kettering, Charles: 61

lack of balanced growth: 49-50
lack of competent advice: 48-49
lack of spontaneity: 6
leading task: 54
lists, making: 30
luck and planning: 52

method, preoccupation with: 7
milestones: 27, 43
models, planning: 9-10
motivation: 58

nature of planning: 5

objectives, defined: 27
obstacles to planning: 8
odds, playing the: 42
opportunities: 16
optimism, excessive: 48
options: 44
organization: 4
orientation, goal: 54
outside-in planning: 9-10
overmotivation: 8
overplanning: 5

Parkinson's Law: 57
patience: 58
performance measures: 36-37
   criteria for: 36
planners, characteristics of
   good: 46-47
   differences between: 47-48
planning, nature of: 5
   benefits of 5-6
   defined: 2-3
   types of: 3
   analytical: 3
   steps in: 3-5
   dangers in: 6-7
   assumptions: 27-28
   obstacles to: 8
planning assumptions: 27-28
planning environment: 42-43
planning models: 9-10
preparation: 4
priorities: 33-35
   assigning: 34-35
problem solving: 2
progress, checking on: 56
psychological distress: 7
   readiness: 41

questions, asking: 30
questions about yourself: 15

readiness, psychological: 41
REJECTION: 15
resources: 44
results, failure to monitor: 50
rewards: 58
risks: 19, 38, 55

self-image: 36
settings: 42-43
simplicity in planning: 45-46
spontaniety, lack of: 6
starting position: 54
starting time: 53
steps in planning: 3-5
stimulating senses: 31
stop, knowing when to: 44
strengths: 11-13

stubbornness: 49
study: 55-56

telephone dial: 19
threats: 16-17
time constraints: 57
time management: 57
types of planning: 3

underplanning: 5
urgency, problems with: 34

vision in planning: 45, 54-55, 63-64

weaknesses: 13
work: 55
Wright Brothers: 5

ORDER FORM

☐ **HOW TO OVERCOME A BAD BACK.** $5.95
A steady favorite among bad-back sufferers and doctors all over the country. It's already sold in eight foreign countries and has become the bible of back pain for millions.

☐ **REJECTION.** $3.95
A great book for the person who's trying to survive rejection and promote acceptance. Bound to be a best seller for sales-people, jobseekers, and lovers. It hits at the heart of the leading cause of anxiety and depression.

☐ **STOP PROCRASTINATING—DO IT!** $2.25
Now in its ninth printing and selling better than ever, following an NBC TODAY show appearance. A perfect book for busy executives, harried homemakers, active college students, or anyone else who wants to get more out of life.

ORDER YOUR BOOKS NOW!
Every order is filled the day it's received. Send check or money order—no cash or c.o.d.—along with 75¢ per copy to cover postage and handling. Minn. residents add 6% sales tax.

Name _____

Address _____

City _____

State/Zip _____

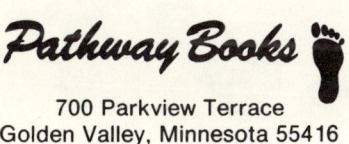

700 Parkview Terrace
Golden Valley, Minnesota 55416